# THE COMPLETE REBEL DIET COOKBOOK

Breaking Food Rules: Satisfying Your Cravings the Rebel Way

CLARE ALLEN

**COPYRIGHT 2025 © CLARE ALLEN**

All rights reserved. No part of this book may be reproduced, stored in retrieval system, or transmitted in any form or by any means, electronic, mechanical, photocopying, recording, or otherwise, without the prior written permission of the copyright holder, except in the case of brief quotations used in critical reviews or articles

# TABLE OF CONTENTS

## Chapter 1 ............................................................................................................... 6
### Introduction to the Rebel Diet ............................................................................. 6
#### Understanding the Rebel Diet Philosophy ........................................................ 6
#### The Benefits of Breaking Traditional Diet Rules ............................................... 6
#### Key Principles of the Rebel Diet ....................................................................... 7
#### Setting Your Own Rules for Success ................................................................ 9
#### Tips for Embracing the Rebel Lifestyle ........................................................... 10

## Chapter 2 ............................................................................................................. 11
### Revolutionary Breakfasts ................................................................................. 11
#### Overnight Oats with a Twist ............................................................................ 11
#### Savory Breakfast Bowls ................................................................................. 12
#### High-Protein Pancakes ................................................................................... 13
#### Rebel Smoothie Creations ............................................................................. 14
#### Avocado and Smoked Salmon Toast ............................................................. 15
#### Rebel Breakfast Burritos ................................................................................ 17

## Chapter 3 ............................................................................................................. 19
### Unconventional Lunches ................................................................................. 19
#### Power-Packed Grain Bowls ........................................................................... 19
#### Creative Salad Jars ....................................................................................... 20
#### Protein-Packed Wraps ................................................................................... 21
#### Rebel Soup Recipes ...................................................................................... 22
#### Stuffed Veggie Creations ............................................................................... 23
#### Low-Carb Lunch Ideas ................................................................................... 25

## Chapter 4 ............................................................................................................. 27
### Daring Dinners ................................................................................................. 27
#### Innovative Stir-Fry Recipes ............................................................................ 27
#### Rebel Pasta Alternatives ................................................................................ 28
#### Grilled Protein with Bold Flavors .................................................................... 29
#### One-Pan Dinner Solutions ............................................................................. 31
#### Rebel Taco Night Ideas .................................................................................. 32
#### Plant-Based Dinner Inspirations .................................................................... 33
#### High-Protein Snack Bars ............................................................................... 35

- Veggie Chips and Dips ... 36
- Rebel Nut Mixes ... 37
- Creative Tapas Plates ... 39
- Savory and Sweet Popcorn Variations ... 40
- Sweet Popcorn Variations ... 41
- Quick and Easy Snack Ideas ... 42

## Chapter 6 ... 44
- Guilt-Free Desserts ... 44
  - Rebel Energy Balls ... 44
  - Healthy Ice Cream Alternatives ... 45
  - Flourless Brownies ... 46
  - No-Bake Dessert Recipes ... 49
  - High-Protein Dessert Creations ... 50

## Chapter 7 ... 52
- Hydration and Beverages ... 52
  - Infused Water Recipes ... 52
  - Rebel Smoothie Blends ... 53
  - Detox Drinks ... 54
  - High-Protein Shakes ... 55
  - Creative Herbal Teas ... 57
  - Low-Calorie Mocktails ... 58

## Chapter 8 ... 59
- Meal Plans and Tips ... 59
  - Weekly Rebel Diet Meal Plan ... 59
  - Budget-Friendly Shopping Tips ... 60
  - Tips for Dining Out on the Rebel Diet ... 62
  - Maintaining Motivation and Consistency ... 62
  - Adapting Recipes to Suit Your Preferences ... 63

## Chapter 9 ... 65
- Success Stories and Testimonials ... 65
  - Inspirational Rebel Diet Journeys ... 65
  - Reader Success Stories ... 66
  - Expert Insights and Advice ... 66

Overcoming Common Challenges .................................................................................. 67
Celebrating Milestones .................................................................................................... 67
Community Support and Resources ................................................................................ 68

# Chapter 1

## Introduction to the Rebel Diet

### Understanding the Rebel Diet Philosophy

Here's a potential introduction to the Rebel Diet Philosophy:

The Rebel Diet Philosophy is a revolutionary approach to weight loss and wellness that rejects the conventional wisdom of traditional dieting. It's a mindset shift, a liberation from the restrictive and unsustainable rules that have held you back from achieving your health goals.

At its core, the Rebel Diet Philosophy is about embracing a more intuitive and flexible approach to eating and living. It's about listening to your body, honoring your cravings, and nourishing yourself with whole, nutrient-dense foods.

This philosophy is not about deprivation or perfection; it's about progress, not perfection. It's about finding a sustainable and enjoyable path to wellness, one that allows you to indulge in your favorite foods, enjoy social gatherings, and live life to the fullest.

By embracing the Rebel Diet Philosophy, you'll learn to:

- Ditch the restrictive rules and guilt-ridden mindset of traditional dieting
- Develop a healthier relationship with food and your body
- Focus on nourishment, not deprivation
- Cultivate self-care and self-love
- Find joy and freedom in your eating and living

Join the rebellion and start your journey to a healthier, happier you!

### The Benefits of Breaking Traditional Diet Rules

Here are some potential benefits of breaking traditional diet rules:

1. Increased Flexibility: Ditching rigid diet rules allows for more flexibility in your eating habits, making it easier to stick to a healthy lifestyle.

2. Reduced Guilt and Shame: Breaking free from traditional diet rules can help alleviate feelings of guilt and shame associated with indulging in "forbidden" foods.

3. Improved Mental Health: Rejecting restrictive dieting can lead to improved mental health, reduced stress, and increased self-esteem.

4. Sustainable Weight Loss: Focusing on nourishment rather than deprivation can lead to sustainable weight loss and improved overall health.

5. Increased Food Enjoyment: Breaking traditional diet rules allows for greater enjoyment of food, reducing the likelihood of feelings of deprivation and increasing satisfaction.

6. Better Nutrient Balance: By not restricting certain food groups, you're more likely to achieve a balanced nutrient intake.

7. More Social Freedom: Ditching diet rules can make social eating and gatherings more enjoyable, reducing anxiety and stress.

8. Increased Self-Trust: Breaking free from traditional diet rules can help you develop a greater trust in your own instincts and ability to make healthy choices.

9. Reduced Obsession with Food: By removing the "good" vs. "bad" food mentality, you can reduce your obsession with food and focus on other aspects of your life.

10. Improved Overall Well-being: Breaking traditional diet rules can lead to improved physical and mental well-being, increased energy, and a greater sense of vitality.

# Key Principles of the Rebel Diet

Here are some potential key principles of the Rebel Diet:

1. Ditch the Rules: Reject restrictive dieting rules and focus on nourishment, not deprivation.

2. Listen to Your Body: Honor your hunger and fullness cues, and eat when and what you want.

3. All Foods Are Allowed: No food is off-limits; enjoy your favorite foods in moderation.

4. Focus on Addition, Not Subtraction: Emphasize adding whole, nutrient-dense foods to your diet, rather than cutting out "bad" foods.

5. Sustainability Over Perfection: Prioritize sustainable, long-term lifestyle changes over short-term, restrictive diets.

6. Self-Care Over Self-Control: Focus on self-care, self-love, and self-acceptance, rather than trying to control your food choices.

7. Intuitive Eating: Eat intuitively, trusting your instincts and listening to your body's hunger and fullness cues.

8. No Guilt, No Shame: Let go of guilt and shame associated with food choices, and focus on nourishment and enjoyment.

9. Focus on Progress, Not Perfection: Celebrate small victories and acknowledge progress, rather than striving for an unattainable ideal.

10. Make Peace with Food: Develop a positive, loving relationship with food, and enjoy the process of nourishing your body.

How to Use This Cookbook
Here's a potential guide on how to use the cookbook:

Welcome to [Cookbook Name]! This cookbook is designed to be your go-to guide for delicious and easy-to-make recipes. Here's how to get the most out of this cookbook:

Before You Start
1. Read the recipe carefully: Before starting to cook, read the recipe from start to finish to ensure you have all the necessary ingredients and equipment.
2. Familiarize yourself with the ingredients: Check the pantry staples and ingredients lists to ensure you have everything you need.

Navigating the Cookbook
1. Recipe chapters: Recipes are organized into chapters by course or ingredient.
2. Recipe format: Each recipe includes a brief introduction, ingredient list, step-by-step instructions, and nutritional information (if applicable).
3. Cooking tips and variations: Many recipes include cooking tips, substitutions, and variations to help you customize the dish to your taste.

Cooking Essentials
1. Kitchen tools and equipment: Make sure you have the necessary kitchen tools and equipment, such as pots, pans, utensils, and appliances.
2. Pantry staples: Stock your pantry with essentials like oils, spices, herbs, and condiments.
3. Ingredient measurements: Use the measurement units specified in each recipe (e.g., cups, grams, tablespoons).

Troubleshooting and Support
1. FAQs: Check the FAQs section for answers to common cooking questions.
2. Online resources: Visit our website or social media channels for additional cooking tips, tutorials, and support.

Happy Cooking!
We hope you enjoy using this cookbook and exploring the world of delicious and easy-to-make recipes. Happy cooking!

# Setting Your Own Rules for Success

Here's a potential guide on setting your own rules for success:

Redefining Success
1. Identify Your Goals: Start by identifying what success means to you. What are your goals and aspirations?
2. Reflect on Your Values: Consider your core values and priorities. What matters most to you in life?

Breaking Free from External Expectations
1. Let Go of Societal Pressure: Release the need to conform to societal standards of success.
2. Dismiss Unrealistic Expectations: Ignore unrealistic expectations from others or yourself.

Creating Your Own Rules
1. Set Personal Standards: Establish personal standards that align with your values and goals.
2. Prioritize Self-Care: Make self-care a non-negotiable part of your daily routine.
3. Focus on Progress, Not Perfection: Celebrate small wins and acknowledge progress, rather than striving for perfection.

Embracing Flexibility and Adaptability
1. Be Open to Change: Remain flexible and adapt to changing circumstances.
2. Learn from Failure: View failures as opportunities for growth and learning.

Maintaining Accountability and Support
1. Surround Yourself with Positive Influences: Build a support network of positive, like-minded individuals.
2. Regularly Assess Progress: Regularly evaluate your progress, celebrating successes and adjusting course as needed.

Conclusion
By setting your own rules for success, you'll be empowered to create a personalized path to achieving your goals. Remember to stay flexible, focused, and true to yourself throughout your journey.

# Tips for Embracing the Rebel Lifestyle

Here are some tips for embracing the Rebel Lifestyle:

Embracing Your Individuality
1. Reject societal norms: Don't conform to societal standards that don't align with your values.
2. Be authentic: Stay true to yourself, even if that means going against the crowd.
3. Celebrate your uniqueness: Embrace what makes you different.

Breaking Free from Restrictions
1. Ditch the rules: Let go of restrictive rules and guidelines that stifle your creativity.
2. Take calculated risks: Step out of your comfort zone and take risks that align with your goals.
3. Embrace freedom: Enjoy the freedom to make choices that align with your values.

Focusing on Self-Care
1. Prioritize self-care: Make self-care a non-negotiable part of your daily routine.
2. Listen to your body: Honor your physical and emotional needs.
3. Practice self-compassion: Treat yourself with kindness and compassion.

Cultivating a Rebel Mindset
1. Challenge the status quo: Question norms and conventions that don't serve you.
2. Think for yourself: Don't blindly follow others; think critically and make informed decisions.
3. Stay curious: Maintain a childlike curiosity and openness to new experiences.

Building a Supportive Community
1. Surround yourself with like-minded individuals: Connect with others who share your values and mindset.
2. Find your tribe: Build a community that supports and encourages you.
3. Lift others up: Support and uplift those around you.

By embracing these tips, you'll be well on your way to living a Rebel Lifestyle that's authentic, empowering, and fulfilling.

# Chapter 2

## Revolutionary Breakfasts

# Overnight Oats with a Twist

Here's a recipe for Overnight Oats with a Twist:

How to Make Overnight Oats with a Twist
Servings: 1
Cooking Time: 0 minutes (refrigerate overnight)
Prep Time: 5 minutes
Total Time: 5 minutes + overnight refrigeration

Nutrition Information (per serving)
- Calories: 250
- Protein: 5g
- Fat: 4g
- Saturated Fat: 0.5g
- Cholesterol: 0mg
- Carbohydrates: 40g
- Fiber: 5g
- Sugar: 15g
- Sodium: 50mg

Ingredients
- 1/2 cup rolled oats
- 1/2 cup unsweetened almond milk
- 1/4 cup plain Greek yogurt
- 1 tablespoon honey or maple syrup
- 1/2 teaspoon vanilla extract
- Pinch of salt
- Toppings:
    - Fresh or dried fruits (e.g., berries, mango, cranberries)
    - Nuts or seeds (e.g., walnuts, almonds, chia seeds)
    - Coconut flakes or shredded coconut
    - Candy pieces or chocolate chips (optional)

Directions
1. In a jar or container, combine the oats, almond milk, Greek yogurt, honey or maple syrup, vanilla extract, and salt. Stir until well combined.
2. Add your desired toppings and stir gently.

3. Cover the jar or container with a lid and refrigerate overnight for at least 4 hours or until morning.
4. In the morning, give the oats a stir and add any additional toppings you like.
5. Serve chilled and enjoy!

Twist Ideas:

- Peanut butter banana: Add mashed banana and peanut butter to the oats.
- Strawberry cheesecake: Add diced strawberries and a drizzle of honey to the oats.
- Mocha: Add instant coffee powder or espresso to the oats.
- Pumpkin spice: Add pumpkin puree, cinnamon, and nutmeg to the oats.

# Savory Breakfast Bowls

Here's a recipe for Savory Breakfast Bowls:

How to Make Savory Breakfast Bowls
Servings: 4
Cooking Time: 20 minutes
Prep Time: 10 minutes
Total Time: 30 minutes

Nutrition Information (per serving)
- Calories: 350
- Protein: 22g
- Fat: 20g
- Saturated Fat: 4g
- Cholesterol: 180mg
- Carbohydrates: 20g
- Fiber: 4g
- Sugar: 2g
- Sodium: 350mg

Ingredients
- 1 cup cooked scrambled eggs
- 1 cup cooked sausage (such as chorizo or breakfast sausage), crumbled
- 1 cup cooked black beans, warmed
- 1 cup diced bell peppers
- 1 cup diced onions
- 2 tablespoons olive oil
- 2 cloves garlic, minced
- 1 teaspoon cumin

- Salt and pepper, to taste
- 4 whole wheat or whole grain tortillas
- Shredded cheese (such as cheddar or Monterey Jack), optional
- Sliced avocado, optional
- Sour cream or Greek yogurt, optional
- Chopped fresh cilantro, optional

Directions
1. In a large skillet, heat the olive oil over medium-high heat. Add the diced onions and cook until translucent, about 3-4 minutes.
2. Add the diced bell peppers to the skillet and cook until tender, about 4-5 minutes.
3. Add the cooked sausage, black beans, cumin, salt, and pepper to the skillet. Stir to combine.
4. Warm the tortillas by wrapping them in a damp paper towel and microwaving for 20-30 seconds.
5. Assemble the breakfast bowls by placing a portion of the scrambled eggs, sausage and bean mixture, and diced vegetables into each tortilla.
6. Top with shredded cheese, sliced avocado, sour cream or Greek yogurt, and chopped cilantro, if desired.
7. Serve immediately and enjoy!

# High-Protein Pancakes

Here's a recipe for High-Protein Pancakes:

How to Make High-Protein Pancakes
Servings: 8-10 pancakes
Cooking Time: 20 minutes
Prep Time: 10 minutes
Total Time: 30 minutes

Nutrition Information (per serving)
- Calories: 250
- Protein: 25g
- Fat: 10g
- Saturated Fat: 2g
- Cholesterol: 100mg
- Carbohydrates: 20g
- Fiber: 2g
- Sugar: 5g
- Sodium: 200mg

Ingredients
- 1 cup rolled oats
- 1/2 cup almond flour
- 1/2 cup protein powder of your choice (e.g., whey, casein, or plant-based)
- 1/4 cup granulated sugar
- 2 teaspoons baking powder
- 1/4 teaspoon salt
- 1 cup unsweetened almond milk
- 1 large egg
- 1 tablespoon melted coconut oil or unsalted butter
- Optional: blueberries, chocolate chips, or other mix-ins of your choice

Directions
1. In a large bowl, combine the oats, almond flour, protein powder, sugar, baking powder, and salt.
2. In a separate bowl, whisk together the almond milk, egg, and melted coconut oil or unsalted butter.
3. Add the wet ingredients to the dry ingredients and stir until just combined. Do not overmix.
4. If using, add your desired mix-ins (e.g., blueberries, chocolate chips) and fold them into the batter.
5. Heat a non-stick skillet or griddle over medium heat.
6. Drop the batter by 1/4 cupfuls onto the skillet or griddle.
7. Cook the pancakes for 2-3 minutes, until bubbles appear on the surface and the edges start to dry.
8. Flip the pancakes and cook for an additional 1-2 minutes, until golden brown.
9. Serve hot and enjoy!

# Rebel Smoothie Creations

Here's a recipe for Rebel Smoothie Creations:

How to Make Rebel Smoothie Creations
Servings: 1
Cooking Time: 0 minutes
Prep Time: 5 minutes
Total Time: 5 minutes

Nutrition Information (per serving)
- Calories: 250-350
- Protein: 20-30g
- Fat: 10-15g
- Saturated Fat: 2-3g
- Cholesterol: 50-100mg
- Carbohydrates: 30-40g
- Fiber: 5-7g

- Sugar: 20-25g
- Sodium: 50-100mg

Ingredients
- 1 cup frozen fruit (e.g., berries, mango, pineapple)
- 1/2 cup plain Greek yogurt
- 1/2 cup unsweetened almond milk
- 1 tablespoon chia seeds
- 1 scoop protein powder (optional)
- 1 teaspoon honey or maple syrup (optional)
- Ice cubes (as needed)
- Toppings (optional): granola, nuts, seeds, fresh fruit

Directions
1. Combine the frozen fruit, Greek yogurt, almond milk, chia seeds, and protein powder (if using) in a blender.
2. Blend the mixture on high speed until smooth and creamy.
3. Add honey or maple syrup (if using) and blend until well combined.
4. Add ice cubes (if needed) and blend until the ice is crushed and the smoothie is the desired consistency.
5. Pour the smoothie into a glass and top with your desired toppings (if using).
6. Serve immediately and enjoy!

Rebel Smoothie Creation Ideas:

- Tropical Temptation: Add pineapple, mango, and coconut flakes to your smoothie.
- Berry Bliss: Blend together frozen mixed berries, Greek yogurt, and almond milk.
- Green Goddess: Add spinach, avocado, and banana to your smoothie.
- Peanut Butter Banana: Blend together frozen banana, peanut butter, and almond milk.
- Mocha Madness: Add instant coffee powder, chocolate protein powder, and almond milk to your smoothie.

# Avocado and Smoked Salmon Toast

Here's a recipe for Avocado and Smoked Salmon Toast:

How to Make Avocado and Smoked Salmon Toast
Servings: 2
Cooking Time: 5 minutes
Prep Time: 5 minutes
Total Time: 10 minutes

Nutrition Information (per serving)
- Calories: 320
- Protein: 20g
- Fat: 22g
- Saturated Fat: 3.5g
- Cholesterol: 20mg
- Carbohydrates: 20g
- Fiber: 7g
- Sugar: 2g
- Sodium: 200mg

Ingredients
- 2 slices whole grain bread (e.g., whole wheat or sourdough)
- 1 ripe avocado, mashed
- 2 slices smoked salmon
- 1 tablespoon freshly squeezed lemon juice
- 1/4 teaspoon salt
- 1/4 teaspoon black pepper
- 1/4 cup thinly sliced red onion
- 1/4 cup capers
- Fresh dill or parsley, chopped (optional)

Directions
1. Toast the bread until lightly browned.
2. Spread the mashed avocado on top of the toast.
3. Place the smoked salmon slices on top of the avocado.
4. Drizzle the lemon juice over the salmon.
5. Sprinkle the salt, black pepper, red onion, and capers over the top.
6. Garnish with chopped fresh dill or parsley, if desired.
7. Serve immediately and enjoy!

Tips and Variations:

- Use high-quality, fresh ingredients for the best flavor.
- Substitute other types of fish, such as trout or tuna, for the smoked salmon.
- Add a sliced egg or a sprinkle of feta cheese for extra protein and flavor.
- Use different types of bread, such as baguette or ciabatta, for a change of pace.

# Rebel Breakfast Burritos

Here's a recipe for Rebel Breakfast Burritos:

How to Make Rebel Breakfast Burritos
Servings: 4-6
Cooking Time: 20 minutes
Prep Time: 10 minutes
Total Time: 30 minutes

Nutrition Information (per serving)
- Calories: 350-400
- Protein: 20-25g
- Fat: 15-20g
- Saturated Fat: 3-4g
- Cholesterol: 150-200mg
- Carbohydrates: 30-35g
- Fiber: 5-7g
- Sugar: 5-7g
- Sodium: 300-400mg

Ingredients
- 6 large eggs
- 1/2 cup diced cooked sausage (e.g., chorizo or breakfast sausage)
- 1/2 cup diced cooked bacon
- 1 cup shredded cheese (e.g., cheddar or Monterey Jack)
- 1 cup canned black beans, drained and rinsed
- 1/2 cup diced bell peppers
- 1/2 cup diced onions
- 6 large tortillas
- Salsa, sour cream, and avocado or guacamole (optional)

Directions
1. In a large skillet, cook the sausage and bacon over medium-high heat until browned.
2. In a separate bowl, whisk together the eggs and a pinch of salt.
3. Add the eggs to the skillet with the cooked sausage and bacon. Scramble the eggs until cooked through.
4. In a separate pan, warm the tortillas over medium heat for about 30 seconds on each side.
5. Assemble the burritos by filling each tortilla with scrambled eggs, cooked sausage and bacon, black beans, bell peppers, onions, and shredded cheese.
6. Add salsa, sour cream, and avocado or guacamole, if desired.
7. Serve immediately and enjoy!

Rebel Variations:

- Add diced ham or cooked chorizo for extra protein.
- Use different types of cheese, such as pepper jack or queso fresco.
- Add diced veggies, such as mushrooms or zucchini.
- Use whole wheat or whole grain tortillas for extra fiber.

# Chapter 3

## Unconventional Lunches

# Power-Packed Grain Bowls

Here's a recipe for Power-Packed Grain Bowls:

How to Make Power-Packed Grain Bowls
Servings: 4-6
Cooking Time: 20-25 minutes
Prep Time: 10-15 minutes
Total Time: 30-40 minutes

Nutrition Information (per serving)
- Calories: 400-500
- Protein: 15-20g
- Fat: 10-15g
- Saturated Fat: 2-3g
- Cholesterol: 0-5mg
- Carbohydrates: 60-70g
- Fiber: 8-10g
- Sugar: 5-7g
- Sodium: 200-300mg

Ingredients
- 1 cup cooked quinoa or brown rice
- 1 cup cooked farro or bulgur
- 1 cup roasted vegetables (e.g., broccoli, sweet potatoes, Brussels sprouts)
- 1 cup mixed greens
- 1/2 cup cooked chickpeas or black beans
- 1/4 cup chopped fresh herbs (e.g., parsley, cilantro, basil)
- 2 tablespoons olive oil
- 1 tablespoon lemon juice
- Salt and pepper, to taste
- Optional: avocado, nuts, seeds, or cheese

Directions
1. Cook the quinoa, farro, or bulgur according to package instructions.
2. Roast the vegetables in the oven with olive oil, salt, and pepper.
3. In a large bowl, combine the cooked grains, roasted vegetables, mixed greens, chickpeas or black beans, and chopped fresh herbs.

4. Drizzle with olive oil and lemon juice, and season with salt and pepper to taste.
5. Top with optional ingredients, such as avocado, nuts, seeds, or cheese.
6. Serve immediately and enjoy!

Power-Packed Variations:

- Add grilled chicken, salmon, or tofu for extra protein.
- Use different types of grains, such as Kamut or spelt.
- Mix in diced fruits, such as apples or berries.
- Add a dollop of yogurt or hummus for extra creaminess.

# Creative Salad Jars

Here's a recipe for Creative Salad Jars:

How to Make Creative Salad Jars
Servings: 4-6
Cooking Time: 0 minutes
Prep Time: 10-15 minutes
Total Time: 10-15 minutes

Nutrition Information (per serving)
- Calories: 150-300
- Protein: 10-20g
- Fat: 5-10g
- Saturated Fat: 1-2g
- Cholesterol: 0-10mg
- Carbohydrates: 10-20g
- Fiber: 5-10g
- Sugar: 5-10g
- Sodium: 100-200mg

Ingredients
- Mixed greens (e.g., arugula, spinach, kale)
- Assorted vegetables (e.g., cherry tomatoes, cucumbers, carrots)
- Protein sources (e.g., grilled chicken, salmon, tofu)
- Cheese or nuts (e.g., feta, parmesan, almonds)
- Seeds (e.g., chia, flax, hemp)
- Salad dressings (e.g., vinaigrette, hummus, ranch)

Directions

1. Choose a jar or container with a wide mouth.
2. Layer the ingredients in the jar, starting with the mixed greens.
3. Add the assorted vegetables, protein sources, cheese or nuts, and seeds.
4. Drizzle with your chosen salad dressing.
5. Top with a lid or plastic wrap and refrigerate for up to 24 hours.
6. Serve chilled and enjoy!

Creative Salad Jar Ideas:

- Southwestern Salad: Add black beans, diced tomatoes, avocado, and a sprinkle of queso fresco.
- Greek Salad: Include feta cheese, olives, cucumber, and a drizzle of Greek vinaigrette.
- Asian-Style Salad: Mix in edamame, sliced almonds, diced mango, and a soy-ginger dressing.
- Autumn Salad: Combine mixed greens, roasted butternut squash, diced apples, and a maple-mustard dressing.

# Protein-Packed Wraps

Here's a recipe for Protein-Packed Wraps:

How to Make Protein-Packed Wraps
Servings: 4-6
Cooking Time: 10-15 minutes
Prep Time: 10-15 minutes
Total Time: 20-30 minutes

Nutrition Information (per serving)
- Calories: 350-450
- Protein: 30-40g
- Fat: 10-15g
- Saturated Fat: 3-5g
- Cholesterol: 60-80mg
- Carbohydrates: 20-25g
- Fiber: 5-7g
- Sugar: 5-7g
- Sodium: 350-450mg

Ingredients
- 1 cup cooked chicken breast or thighs
- 1/2 cup cooked black beans or chickpeas
- 1/2 cup diced bell peppers
- 1/2 cup diced cucumber

- 1/4 cup crumbled feta cheese or goat cheese
- 1 tablespoon hummus or avocado spread
- 1 large flour tortilla or whole wheat wrap
- Mixed greens or spinach
- Optional: sliced avocado, sliced olives, pickled jalapeños

Directions
1. Cook the chicken breast or thighs according to your preference.
2. In a large bowl, combine the cooked chicken, black beans or chickpeas, diced bell peppers, and diced cucumber.
3. In a small bowl, mix together the hummus or avocado spread and crumbled feta cheese or goat cheese.
4. Spread the hummus or avocado mixture onto the tortilla or wrap.
5. Add the chicken and vegetable mixture on top of the hummus or avocado spread.
6. Add mixed greens or spinach and any optional toppings.
7. Roll up the wrap tightly and slice in half.
8. Serve immediately and enjoy!

Protein-Packed Wrap Variations:

- Mediterranean Wrap: Add sliced olives, artichoke hearts, and a sprinkle of feta cheese.
- Southwestern Wrap: Include diced chicken, black beans, diced tomatoes, and a drizzle of salsa.
- Italian Wrap: Mix in sliced ham, salami, pepperoni, and a sprinkle of parmesan cheese.
- Veggie Wrap: Add roasted vegetables, hummus, and mixed greens.

# Rebel Soup Recipes

Here's a recipe for Rebel Soup Recipes:

How to Make Rebel Soup Recipes
Servings: 4-6
Cooking Time: 30-40 minutes
Prep Time: 15-20 minutes
Total Time: 45-60 minutes

Nutrition Information (per serving)
- Calories: 200-300
- Protein: 15-20g
- Fat: 10-15g
- Saturated Fat: 2-3g
- Cholesterol: 40-60mg

- Carbohydrates: 20-25g
- Fiber: 5-7g
- Sugar: 5-7g
- Sodium: 400-600mg

Ingredients
- 2 tablespoons olive oil
- 1 onion, diced
- 3 cloves garlic, minced
- 1 teaspoon ground cumin
- 1 teaspoon smoked paprika
- 1/2 teaspoon cayenne pepper
- 1 can (14.5 oz) diced tomatoes
- 4 cups vegetable broth
- 1 can (15 oz) kidney beans, drained and rinsed
- Salt and pepper, to taste
- Optional: avocado, sour cream, shredded cheese, diced onions

Directions
1. Heat the olive oil in a large pot over medium heat.
2. Add the diced onion and cook until softened, about 5 minutes.
3. Add the minced garlic and cook for an additional minute.
4. Stir in the cumin, smoked paprika, and cayenne pepper.
5. Add the diced tomatoes, vegetable broth, and kidney beans.
6. Bring the mixture to a boil, then reduce the heat and simmer for 20-25 minutes.
7. Season with salt and pepper to taste.
8. Serve hot, with optional toppings such as avocado, sour cream, shredded cheese, and diced onions.

Rebel Soup Variations:

- Spicy Black Bean Soup: Add diced jalapeños and a sprinkle of cumin.
- Creamy Tomato Soup: Blend in heavy cream or coconut cream for a creamy texture.
- Roasted Vegetable Soup: Add roasted vegetables such as carrots, zucchini, and bell peppers.
- Lentil Soup: Substitute lentils for the kidney beans and add diced spinach.

# Stuffed Veggie Creations

Here's a recipe for Stuffed Veggie Creations:

How to Make Stuffed Veggie Creations
Servings: 4-6

Cooking Time: 25-35 minutes
Prep Time: 15-20 minutes
Total Time: 40-55 minutes

Nutrition Information (per serving)
- Calories: 150-200
- Protein: 5-10g
- Fat: 5-10g
- Saturated Fat: 1-2g
- Cholesterol: 0-5mg
- Carbohydrates: 20-25g
- Fiber: 5-7g
- Sugar: 5-7g
- Sodium: 100-200mg

Ingredients
- 4-6 bell peppers, any color
- 1 cup cooked rice
- 1 cup black beans, cooked
- 1 cup diced tomatoes
- 1/2 cup shredded cheese
- 1/4 cup chopped fresh cilantro
- 1 tablespoon olive oil
- Salt and pepper, to taste
- Optional: ground beef, turkey, or veggies for added protein

Directions
1. Preheat oven to 375°F (190°C).
2. Cut off the tops of the bell peppers and remove seeds and membranes.
3. In a large bowl, mix together cooked rice, black beans, diced tomatoes, shredded cheese, and chopped cilantro.
4. Stuff each bell pepper with the rice mixture and top with olive oil.
5. Place the bell peppers in a baking dish and bake for 25-35 minutes, or until tender.
6. Serve hot and enjoy!

Stuffed Veggie Creation Variations:

- Mexican Stuffed Peppers: Add diced jalapeños, salsa, and avocado.
- Italian Stuffed Peppers: Mix in chopped olives, artichoke hearts, and parmesan cheese.
- Vegan Stuffed Peppers: Replace cheese with nutritional yeast and add roasted vegetables.
- Protein-Packed Stuffed Peppers: Add cooked ground beef, turkey, or chicken for extra protein.

# Low-Carb Lunch Ideas

Here are some delicious Low-Carb Lunch Ideas:

Low-Carb Lunch Ideas
1. Turkey Lettuce Wraps
Servings: 1
Cooking Time: 5 minutes
Prep Time: 5 minutes
Total Time: 10 minutes
- Calories: 350
- Protein: 30g
- Fat: 20g
- Carbohydrates: 5g

2. Tuna Salad
Servings: 1
Cooking Time: 0 minutes
Prep Time: 5 minutes
Total Time: 5 minutes
- Calories: 300
- Protein: 30g
- Fat: 20g
- Carbohydrates: 5g

3. Chicken Caesar Salad
Servings: 1
Cooking Time: 10 minutes
Prep Time: 5 minutes
Total Time: 15 minutes
- Calories: 350
- Protein: 35g
- Fat: 25g
- Carbohydrates: 5g

4. Zucchini Boats
Servings: 1
Cooking Time: 15 minutes
Prep Time: 10 minutes
Total Time: 25 minutes
- Calories: 200
- Protein: 15g
- Fat: 15g

- Carbohydrates: 5g

5. Cobb Salad
Servings: 1
Cooking Time: 10 minutes
Prep Time: 5 minutes
Total Time: 15 minutes
- Calories: 350
- Protein: 30g
- Fat: 25g
- Carbohydrates: 5g

Ingredients and Directions for Each Recipe
Turkey Lettuce Wraps
- Ingredients: 2 oz turkey breast, 1 cup lettuce, 1/2 cup avocado, 1/4 cup tomato
- Directions: Slice turkey breast, layer with lettuce, avocado, and tomato in a lettuce wrap

Tuna Salad
- Ingredients: 6 oz canned tuna, 1/4 cup mayonnaise, 1/4 cup chopped onion
- Directions: Mix tuna, mayonnaise, and chopped onion in a bowl

Chicken Caesar Salad
- Ingredients: 4 oz grilled chicken, 2 cups romaine lettuce, 1/4 cup Caesar dressing
- Directions: Grill chicken, toss with romaine lettuce and Caesar dressing

Zucchini Boats
- Ingredients: 2 medium zucchinis, 2 oz ground turkey, 1/4 cup grated cheese
- Directions: Hollow out zucchinis, fill with ground turkey and cheese, bake until tender

Cobb Salad
- Ingredients: 4 oz grilled chicken, 2 cups mixed greens, 1/2 cup chopped bacon, 1/2 cup chopped avocado
- Directions: Grill chicken, toss with mixed greens, chopped bacon, and chopped avocado

These low-carb lunch ideas are quick, easy, and delicious!

# Chapter 4

## Daring Dinners

# Innovative Stir-Fry Recipes

Here are some Innovative Stir-Fry Recipes:

How to Make Innovative Stir-Fries
Servings: 4-6
Cooking Time: 15-25 minutes
Prep Time: 10-15 minutes
Total Time: 25-40 minutes

Nutrition Information (per serving)
- Calories: 250-350
- Protein: 20-30g
- Fat: 10-15g
- Saturated Fat: 2-3g
- Cholesterol: 60-80mg
- Carbohydrates: 20-25g
- Fiber: 5-7g
- Sugar: 5-7g
- Sodium: 400-600mg

Ingredients
- 2 tablespoons vegetable oil
- 1 onion, sliced
- 2 cloves garlic, minced
- 1 cup mixed vegetables (e.g., bell peppers, carrots, broccoli)
- 1 cup cooked protein (e.g., chicken, beef, tofu)
- 2 teaspoons soy sauce
- 1 teaspoon oyster sauce (optional)
- Salt and pepper, to taste
- Optional: nuts, seeds, or dried fruit

Directions
1. Heat the vegetable oil in a large skillet or wok over medium-high heat.
2. Add the sliced onion and cook until softened, about 3-4 minutes.
3. Add the minced garlic and cook for an additional minute.
4. Add the mixed vegetables and cooked protein, and stir-fry until the vegetables are tender-crisp.
5. In a small bowl, whisk together the soy sauce and oyster sauce (if using).

6. Pour the sauce over the stir-fry and stir to combine.
7. Season with salt and pepper to taste.
8. Serve hot, garnished with nuts, seeds, or dried fruit (if desired).

Innovative Stir-Fry Variations:

- Korean BBQ Stir-Fry: Add gochujang (Korean chili paste) and soy sauce to the stir-fry.
- Thai Peanut Stir-Fry: Mix in peanut butter, soy sauce, and honey for a creamy and spicy sauce.
- Indian-Style Stir-Fry: Add curry powder and cumin to the stir-fry, and serve with naan bread or basmati rice.
- Japanese Teriyaki Stir-Fry: Mix in teriyaki sauce and sesame oil for a sweet and savory flavor.

# Rebel Pasta Alternatives

Here are some Rebel Pasta Alternatives:

Zucchini Noodles (Zoodles)
- Calories: 25-50 per cup
- Protein: 1-2g
- Fat: 0-1g
- Carbohydrates: 6-10g
- Fiber: 2-3g

Spaghetti Squash
- Calories: 40-60 per cup
- Protein: 1-2g
- Fat: 0-1g
- Carbohydrates: 10-15g
- Fiber: 2-3g

Shirataki Noodles
- Calories: 5-10 per cup
- Protein: 1-2g
- Fat: 0-1g
- Carbohydrates: 5-10g
- Fiber: 2-3g

Vegetable Ribbons
- Calories: 20-40 per cup
- Protein: 1-2g
- Fat: 0-1g

- Carbohydrates: 5-10g
- Fiber: 2-3g

How to Prepare Rebel Pasta Alternatives
1. Zoodles: Use a spiralizer to create zucchini noodles. Sauté with olive oil, garlic, and your favorite sauce.
2. Spaghetti Squash: Bake or microwave spaghetti squash until tender. Use a fork to shred into strands.
3. Shirataki Noodles: Rinse and cook shirataki noodles according to package instructions. Top with your favorite sauce.
4. Vegetable Ribbons: Use a peeler or spiralizer to create ribbons from carrots, beets, or parsnips. Sauté with olive oil and your favorite seasonings.

Rebel Pasta Alternative Recipes:

- Zoodle Bolognese: Toss zoodles with ground beef, tomato sauce, and parmesan cheese.
- Spaghetti Squash Carbonara: Toss spaghetti squash with bacon, eggs, and parmesan cheese.
- Shirataki Noodle Stir-Fry: Stir-fry shirataki noodles with vegetables, soy sauce, and sesame oil.
- Vegetable Ribbon Salad: Toss vegetable ribbons with mixed greens, cherry tomatoes, and a homemade vinaigrette.

# Grilled Protein with Bold Flavors

Here are some Grilled Protein with Bold Flavors recipes:

Grilled Chicken Shawarma
- Servings: 4-6
- Cooking Time: 10-15 minutes
- Prep Time: 10-15 minutes
- Calories: 350-400
- Protein: 35-40g
- Fat: 15-20g
- Carbohydrates: 10-15g

Grilled Steak Fajitas
- Servings: 4-6
- Cooking Time: 10-15 minutes
- Prep Time: 10-15 minutes
- Calories: 400-500
- Protein: 40-50g
- Fat: 20-25g

- Carbohydrates: 10-15g

Grilled Salmon with Lemon-Herb Butter
- Servings: 4-6
- Cooking Time: 8-12 minutes
- Prep Time: 5-10 minutes
- Calories: 300-350
- Protein: 30-35g
- Fat: 15-20g
- Carbohydrates: 0-5g

Grilled Shrimp Skewers with Spicy Mango Sauce
- Servings: 4-6
- Cooking Time: 8-12 minutes
- Prep Time: 10-15 minutes
- Calories: 200-250
- Protein: 20-25g
- Fat: 10-15g
- Carbohydrates: 10-15g

Ingredients and Directions for Each Recipe
- Grilled Chicken Shawarma:
    - Ingredients: chicken breast, olive oil, lemon juice, garlic, oregano, salt, pepper
    - Directions: Marinate chicken in olive oil, lemon juice, garlic, and oregano. Grill chicken and serve in pita bread with tzatziki sauce.
- Grilled Steak Fajitas:
    - Ingredients: steak, olive oil, lime juice, garlic, cumin, chili powder, salt, pepper
    - Directions: Marinate steak in olive oil, lime juice, garlic, cumin, and chili powder. Grill steak and serve with sautéed onions and bell peppers.
- Grilled Salmon with Lemon-Herb Butter:
    - Ingredients: salmon fillet, lemon juice, butter, parsley, dill, salt, pepper
    - Directions: Mix lemon juice, butter, parsley, and dill. Grill salmon and top with lemon-herb butter.
- Grilled Shrimp Skewers with Spicy Mango Sauce:
    - Ingredients: shrimp, mango, red pepper flakes, olive oil, lime juice, salt, pepper
    - Directions: Marinate shrimp in olive oil, lime juice, and red pepper flakes. Grill shrimp and serve with spicy mango sauce.

# One-Pan Dinner Solutions

Here are some delicious One-Pan Dinner Solutions:

Chicken Fajita One-Pan Dinner
- Servings: 4-6
- Cooking Time: 20-25 minutes
- Prep Time: 10-15 minutes
- Calories: 350-400
- Protein: 30-35g
- Fat: 15-20g
- Carbohydrates: 20-25g

Baked Chicken and Sweet Potato One-Pan Dinner
- Servings: 4-6
- Cooking Time: 30-35 minutes
- Prep Time: 10-15 minutes
- Calories: 300-350
- Protein: 25-30g
- Fat: 10-15g
- Carbohydrates: 30-35g

One-Pan Pasta with Tomatoes and Basil
- Servings: 4-6
- Cooking Time: 15-20 minutes
- Prep Time: 5-10 minutes
- Calories: 250-300
- Protein: 15-20g
- Fat: 10-15g
- Carbohydrates: 30-35g

Chicken and Broccoli One-Pan Stir-Fry
- Servings: 4-6
- Cooking Time: 15-20 minutes
- Prep Time: 5-10 minutes
- Calories: 200-250
- Protein: 20-25g
- Fat: 10-15g
- Carbohydrates: 10-15g

Ingredients and Directions for Each Recipe
- Chicken Fajita One-Pan Dinner:
    - Ingredients: chicken breast, bell peppers, onions, fajita seasoning, tortillas

- Directions: Cook chicken and vegetables in a large skillet with fajita seasoning. Serve with tortillas.
- Baked Chicken and Sweet Potato One-Pan Dinner:
   - Ingredients: chicken breast, sweet potatoes, olive oil, salt, pepper
   - Directions: Bake chicken and sweet potatoes in the oven with olive oil and seasoning.
- One-Pan Pasta with Tomatoes and Basil:
   - Ingredients: pasta, cherry tomatoes, basil, olive oil, garlic
   - Directions: Cook pasta, cherry tomatoes, and basil in a large skillet with olive oil and garlic.
- Chicken and Broccoli One-Pan Stir-Fry:
   - Ingredients: chicken breast, broccoli, olive oil, soy sauce, garlic
   - Directions: Cook chicken and broccoli in a large skillet with olive oil, soy sauce, and garlic.

# Rebel Taco Night Ideas

Here are some delicious Rebel Taco Night Ideas:

Korean BBQ Tacos
- Servings: 4-6
- Cooking Time: 15-20 minutes
- Prep Time: 10-15 minutes
- Calories: 300-350
- Protein: 20-25g
- Fat: 15-20g
- Carbohydrates: 20-25g

Baja-Style Fish Tacos
- Servings: 4-6
- Cooking Time: 10-15 minutes
- Prep Time: 10-15 minutes
- Calories: 250-300
- Protein: 20-25g
- Fat: 10-15g
- Carbohydrates: 15-20g

Vegan Black Bean and Sweet Potato Tacos
- Servings: 4-6
- Cooking Time: 20-25 minutes
- Prep Time: 10-15 minutes
- Calories: 250-300
- Protein: 10-15g
- Fat: 10-15g

- Carbohydrates: 30-35g

Breakfast Tacos with Scrambled Eggs and Chorizo
- Servings: 4-6
- Cooking Time: 10-15 minutes
- Prep Time: 5-10 minutes
- Calories: 250-300
- Protein: 15-20g
- Fat: 15-20g
- Carbohydrates: 10-15g

Ingredients and Directions for Each Recipe
- Korean BBQ Tacos:
    - Ingredients: ground beef, Korean chili flakes, soy sauce, lime juice, cilantro
    - Directions: Cook ground beef with Korean chili flakes and soy sauce. Serve in tacos with lime juice and cilantro.
- Baja-Style Fish Tacos:
    - Ingredients: cod, lime juice, cumin, chili powder, cabbage
    - Directions: Cook cod with lime juice and spices. Serve in tacos with cabbage and salsa.
- Vegan Black Bean and Sweet Potato Tacos:
    - Ingredients: black beans, sweet potatoes, cumin, chili powder, avocado
    - Directions: Cook black beans and sweet potatoes with cumin and chili powder. Serve in tacos with avocado and salsa.
- Breakfast Tacos with Scrambled Eggs and Chorizo:
    - Ingredients: scrambled eggs, chorizo, tortillas, shredded cheese
    - Directions: Cook scrambled eggs and chorizo. Serve in tacos with tortillas and shredded cheese.

# Plant-Based Dinner Inspirations

Here are some delicious Plant-Based Dinner Inspiration ideas:

Lentil and Mushroom Curry
- Servings: 4-6
- Cooking Time: 30-40 minutes
- Prep Time: 15-20 minutes
- Calories: 400-500
- Protein: 20-25g
- Fat: 10-15g
- Carbohydrates: 60-70g

Roasted Vegetable Quinoa Bowl

- Servings: 4-6
- Cooking Time: 25-35 minutes
- Prep Time: 10-15 minutes
- Calories: 350-450
- Protein: 15-20g
- Fat: 10-15g
- Carbohydrates: 50-60g

Vegan Black Bean and Sweet Potato Enchiladas
- Servings: 4-6
- Cooking Time: 30-40 minutes
- Prep Time: 15-20 minutes
- Calories: 400-500
- Protein: 20-25g
- Fat: 10-15g
- Carbohydrates: 60-70g

Grilled Portobello Mushroom Burgers
- Servings: 4-6
- Cooking Time: 10-15 minutes
- Prep Time: 10-15 minutes
- Calories: 250-350
- Protein: 15-20g
- Fat: 10-15g
- Carbohydrates: 20-25g

Ingredients and Directions for Each Recipe
- Lentil and Mushroom Curry:
    - Ingredients: lentils, mushrooms, onion, garlic, curry powder, coconut milk
    - Directions: Cook lentils and mushrooms in a curry sauce made with coconut milk and spices.
- Roasted Vegetable Quinoa Bowl:
    - Ingredients: quinoa, roasted vegetables (e.g., broccoli, carrots, sweet potatoes), lemon juice, olive oil
    - Directions: Cook quinoa and roast vegetables in the oven with lemon juice and olive oil.
- Vegan Black Bean and Sweet Potato Enchiladas:
    - Ingredients: black beans, sweet potatoes, enchilada sauce, tortillas, vegan cheese
    - Directions: Cook black beans and sweet potatoes, then fill tortillas with the mixture and bake with enchilada sauce and vegan cheese.
- Grilled Portobello Mushroom Burgers:
    - Ingredients: portobello mushrooms, buns, lettuce, tomato, vegan mayo
    - Directions: Grill portobello mushrooms and serve on a bun with lettuce, tomato, and vegan mayo.

Chapter 5: Satisfying Snacks and Appetizers

# High-Protein Snack Bars

Here are some High-Protein Snack Bar recipes:

Peanut Butter Banana Protein Bars
- Servings: 12-16 bars
- Cooking Time: 10-15 minutes
- Prep Time: 5-10 minutes
- Calories: 200-250 per bar
- Protein: 15-20g
- Fat: 8-10g
- Carbohydrates: 20-25g

Chocolate Chip Coconut Protein Bars
- Servings: 12-16 bars
- Cooking Time: 10-15 minutes
- Prep Time: 5-10 minutes
- Calories: 220-270 per bar
- Protein: 15-20g
- Fat: 10-12g
- Carbohydrates: 25-30g

Cinnamon Apple Protein Bars
- Servings: 12-16 bars
- Cooking Time: 10-15 minutes
- Prep Time: 5-10 minutes
- Calories: 200-250 per bar
- Protein: 15-20g
- Fat: 8-10g
- Carbohydrates: 20-25g

No-Bake Energy Protein Bars
- Servings: 12-16 bars
- Cooking Time: 0 minutes
- Prep Time: 5-10 minutes
- Calories: 200-250 per bar
- Protein: 15-20g
- Fat: 8-10g
- Carbohydrates: 20-25g

Ingredients and Directions for Each Recipe
- Peanut Butter Banana Protein Bars:
    - Ingredients: rolled oats, peanut butter, banana, protein powder, honey

- Directions: Mix all ingredients in a bowl until well combined. Press into a baking dish and refrigerate until set.
- Chocolate Chip Coconut Protein Bars:
  - Ingredients: rolled oats, coconut flakes, protein powder, chocolate chips, honey
  - Directions: Mix all ingredients in a bowl until well combined. Press into a baking dish and refrigerate until set.
- Cinnamon Apple Protein Bars:
  - Ingredients: rolled oats, protein powder, cinnamon, apple, honey
  - Directions: Mix all ingredients in a bowl until well combined. Press into a baking dish and refrigerate until set.
- No-Bake Energy Protein Bars:
  - Ingredients: rolled oats, protein powder, nut butter, honey
  - Directions: Mix all ingredients in a bowl until well combined. Press into a baking dish and refrigerate until set.

# Veggie Chips and Dips

Here are some delicious Veggie Chips and Dips recipes:

Baked Sweet Potato Chips with Spicy Hummus
- Servings: 4-6
- Cooking Time: 20-25 minutes
- Prep Time: 10-15 minutes
- Calories: 150-200 per serving
- Protein: 5-7g
- Fat: 10-12g
- Carbohydrates: 20-25g

Kale Chips with Lemon-Tahini Dip
- Servings: 4-6
- Cooking Time: 10-15 minutes
- Prep Time: 5-10 minutes
- Calories: 100-150 per serving
- Protein: 3-5g
- Fat: 10-12g
- Carbohydrates: 10-15g

Carrot and Ginger Chips with Avocado Ranch Dip
- Servings: 4-6
- Cooking Time: 20-25 minutes

- Prep Time: 10-15 minutes
- Calories: 150-200 per serving
- Protein: 5-7g
- Fat: 10-12g
- Carbohydrates: 20-25g

Beet Chips with Garlic and Herb Dip
- Servings: 4-6
- Cooking Time: 20-25 minutes
- Prep Time: 10-15 minutes
- Calories: 100-150 per serving
- Protein: 3-5g
- Fat: 10-12g
- Carbohydrates: 15-20g

Ingredients and Directions for Each Recipe
- Baked Sweet Potato Chips with Spicy Hummus:
    - Ingredients: sweet potatoes, olive oil, salt, hummus, cumin, chili powder
    - Directions: Bake sweet potato slices in the oven until crispy. Serve with spicy hummus.
- Kale Chips with Lemon-Tahini Dip:
    - Ingredients: kale, olive oil, salt, lemon juice, tahini, garlic
    - Directions: Bake kale leaves in the oven until crispy. Serve with lemon-tahini dip.
- Carrot and Ginger Chips with Avocado Ranch Dip:
    - Ingredients: carrots, ginger, olive oil, salt, avocado, ranch seasoning
    - Directions: Bake carrot and ginger slices in the oven until crispy. Serve with avocado ranch dip.
- Beet Chips with Garlic and Herb Dip:
    - Ingredients: beets, olive oil, salt, garlic, herbs (e.g., parsley, dill)
    - Directions: Bake beet slices in the oven until crispy. Serve with garlic and herb dip.

# Rebel Nut Mixes

Here are some delicious Rebel Nut Mixes recipes:

Spicy Tex-Mex Nut Mix
- Servings: 4-6
- Prep Time: 5 minutes
- Calories: 150-200 per 1/4 cup serving
- Protein: 5-7g
- Fat: 12-15g
- Carbohydrates: 10-12g

Indian-Style Curry Nut Mix
- Servings: 4-6
- Prep Time: 5 minutes
- Calories: 150-200 per 1/4 cup serving
- Protein: 5-7g
- Fat: 12-15g
- Carbohydrates: 10-12g

Sweet and Salty Chocolate Nut Mix
- Servings: 4-6
- Prep Time: 5 minutes
- Calories: 150-200 per 1/4 cup serving
- Protein: 5-7g
- Fat: 12-15g
- Carbohydrates: 15-18g

Mediterranean Herb Nut Mix
- Servings: 4-6
- Prep Time: 5 minutes
- Calories: 150-200 per 1/4 cup serving
- Protein: 5-7g
- Fat: 12-15g
- Carbohydrates: 10-12g

Ingredients and Directions for Each Recipe
- Spicy Tex-Mex Nut Mix:
    - Ingredients: almonds, pecans, chili powder, cumin, smoked paprika, salt
    - Directions: Mix all ingredients in a bowl until well combined.
- Indian-Style Curry Nut Mix:
    - Ingredients: cashews, pistachios, curry powder, garam masala, cumin, salt
    - Directions: Mix all ingredients in a bowl until well combined.
- Sweet and Salty Chocolate Nut Mix:
    - Ingredients: almonds, pecans, chocolate chips, sea salt
    - Directions: Mix all ingredients in a bowl until well combined.
- Mediterranean Herb Nut Mix:
    - Ingredients: almonds, pistachios, dried oregano, thyme, rosemary, salt
    - Directions: Mix all ingredients in a bowl until well combined.

# Creative Tapas Plates

Here are some Creative Tapas Plates ideas:

Grilled Shrimp Skewers with Spicy Mango Sauce
- Servings: 4-6
- Cooking Time: 8-12 minutes
- Prep Time: 10-15 minutes
- Calories: 120-150 per serving
- Protein: 15-20g
- Fat: 2-3g
- Carbohydrates: 10-12g

Patatas Bravas with Spicy Aioli
- Servings: 4-6
- Cooking Time: 15-20 minutes
- Prep Time: 10-15 minutes
- Calories: 150-200 per serving
- Protein: 2-3g
- Fat: 10-12g
- Carbohydrates: 20-25g

Crostini with Fig Jam, Prosciutto, and Arugula
- Servings: 4-6
- Cooking Time: 5-10 minutes
- Prep Time: 10-15 minutes
- Calories: 100-150 per serving
- Protein: 5-7g
- Fat: 5-7g
- Carbohydrates: 15-20g

Pan-Seared Chorizo with Roasted Red Pepper Sauce
- Servings: 4-6
- Cooking Time: 10-15 minutes
- Prep Time: 10-15 minutes
- Calories: 150-200 per serving
- Protein: 10-15g
- Fat: 10-12g
- Carbohydrates: 5-7g

Ingredients and Directions for Each Recipe
- Grilled Shrimp Skewers with Spicy Mango Sauce:
    - Ingredients: shrimp, mango, red pepper flakes, olive oil, lime juice

- Directions: Grill shrimp skewers and serve with spicy mango sauce.
- Patatas Bravas with Spicy Aioli:
    - Ingredients: potatoes, olive oil, garlic, smoked paprika, aioli
    - Directions: Fry potato cubes and serve with spicy aioli.
- Crostini with Fig Jam, Prosciutto, and Arugula:
    - Ingredients: baguette, fig jam, prosciutto, arugula
    - Directions: Top toasted baguette slices with fig jam, prosciutto, and arugula.
- Pan-Seared Chorizo with Roasted Red Pepper Sauce:
    - Ingredients: chorizo, red peppers, olive oil, garlic
    - Directions: Pan-sear chorizo and serve with roasted red pepper sauce.

# Savory and Sweet Popcorn Variations

Here are some Savory and Sweet Popcorn Variations:

Savory Popcorn Variations

Cheesy Garlic Popcorn
- Servings: 4-6
- Prep Time: 5 minutes
- Calories: 120-150 per serving
- Protein: 2-3g
- Fat: 7-9g
- Carbohydrates: 15-20g

Spicy Paprika Popcorn
- Servings: 4-6
- Prep Time: 5 minutes
- Calories: 100-120 per serving
- Protein: 2-3g
- Fat: 5-7g
- Carbohydrates: 15-20g

Herb and Lemon Popcorn
- Servings: 4-6
- Prep Time: 5 minutes
- Calories: 100-120 per serving
- Protein: 2-3g
- Fat: 5-7g
- Carbohydrates: 15-20g

# Sweet Popcorn Variations

Caramel Popcorn with Sea Salt
- Servings: 4-6
- Prep Time: 10 minutes
- Calories: 150-180 per serving
- Protein: 2-3g
- Fat: 9-11g
- Carbohydrates: 25-30g

Chocolate Mint Popcorn
- Servings: 4-6
- Prep Time: 10 minutes
- Calories: 150-180 per serving
- Protein: 2-3g
- Fat: 9-11g
- Carbohydrates: 25-30g

Cinnamon Sugar Popcorn
- Servings: 4-6
- Prep Time: 5 minutes
- Calories: 100-120 per serving
- Protein: 2-3g
- Fat: 5-7g
- Carbohydrates: 20-25g

Ingredients and Directions for Each Recipe
- Cheesy Garlic Popcorn:
    - Ingredients: popcorn kernels, butter, garlic powder, cheddar cheese
    - Directions: Pop popcorn kernels and mix with melted butter, garlic powder, and cheddar cheese.
- Spicy Paprika Popcorn:
    - Ingredients: popcorn kernels, olive oil, smoked paprika, salt
    - Directions: Pop popcorn kernels and mix with olive oil, smoked paprika, and salt.
- Herb and Lemon Popcorn:
    - Ingredients: popcorn kernels, olive oil, lemon zest, chopped herbs (e.g., parsley, dill)
    - Directions: Pop popcorn kernels and mix with olive oil, lemon zest, and chopped herbs.
- Caramel Popcorn with Sea Salt:
    - Ingredients: popcorn kernels, light corn syrup, brown sugar, butter, sea salt
    - Directions: Pop popcorn kernels and mix with melted caramel sauce and sea salt.
- Chocolate Mint Popcorn:
    - Ingredients: popcorn kernels, melted chocolate, peppermint extract, crushed candy canes (optional)
    - Directions: Pop popcorn kernels and mix with melted chocolate, peppermint extract, and crushed candy canes (if using).

- Cinnamon Sugar Popcorn:
    - Ingredients: popcorn kernels, granulated sugar, cinnamon
    - Directions: Pop popcorn kernels and mix with granulated sugar and cinnamon.

# Quick and Easy Snack Ideas

Here are some Quick and Easy Snack Ideas:

Fresh Fruit Kebabs
- Servings: 4-6
- Prep Time: 5 minutes
- Calories: 60-80 per serving
- Protein: 1-2g
- Fat: 0-1g
- Carbohydrates: 15-20g

Yogurt Parfait
- Servings: 1-2
- Prep Time: 5 minutes
- Calories: 150-200 per serving
- Protein: 10-15g
- Fat: 0-5g
- Carbohydrates: 20-25g

Hummus and Veggie Sticks
- Servings: 4-6
- Prep Time: 5 minutes
- Calories: 100-150 per serving
- Protein: 5-7g
- Fat: 10-12g
- Carbohydrates: 10-15g

Energy Balls
- Servings: 12-15
- Prep Time: 10 minutes
- Calories: 100-120 per serving
- Protein: 2-3g
- Fat: 5-7g
- Carbohydrates: 15-20g

Trail Mix

- Servings: 4-6
- Prep Time: 5 minutes
- Calories: 150-200 per serving
- Protein: 5-7g
- Fat: 10-12g
- Carbohydrates: 20-25g

Ingredients and Directions for Each Recipe
- Fresh Fruit Kebabs:
    - Ingredients: fresh fruit (e.g., grapes, strawberries, pineapple), wooden skewers
    - Directions: Thread fresh fruit onto wooden skewers.
- Yogurt Parfait:
    - Ingredients: yogurt, granola, fresh fruit (e.g., berries, banana)
    - Directions: Layer yogurt, granola, and fresh fruit in a bowl.
- Hummus and Veggie Sticks:
    - Ingredients: hummus, carrot sticks, celery sticks, cucumber slices
    - Directions: Serve hummus with veggie sticks.
- Energy Balls:
    - Ingredients: rolled oats, nut butter, honey, chocolate chips
    - Directions: Mix all ingredients in a bowl until well combined. Roll into balls.
- Trail Mix:
    - Ingredients: nuts (e.g., almonds, cashews), dried fruit (e.g., cranberries, raisins), chocolate chips
    - Directions: Mix all ingredients in a bowl until well combined.

# Chapter 6

## Guilt-Free Desserts

# Rebel Energy Balls

Here are some Rebel Energy Balls recipes:

Peanut Butter Banana Energy Balls
- Servings: 12-15
- Prep Time: 10 minutes
- Calories: 120-150 per serving
- Protein: 4-5g
- Fat: 8-10g
- Carbohydrates: 15-20g

Chocolate Chip Coconut Energy Balls
- Servings: 12-15
- Prep Time: 10 minutes
- Calories: 150-180 per serving
- Protein: 3-4g
- Fat: 10-12g
- Carbohydrates: 20-25g

Cinnamon Apple Energy Balls
- Servings: 12-15
- Prep Time: 10 minutes
- Calories: 100-120 per serving
- Protein: 2-3g
- Fat: 5-7g
- Carbohydrates: 20-25g

Pumpkin Spice Energy Balls
- Servings: 12-15
- Prep Time: 10 minutes
- Calories: 120-150 per serving
- Protein: 3-4g
- Fat: 8-10g
- Carbohydrates: 20-25g

Ingredients and Directions for Each Recipe
- Peanut Butter Banana Energy Balls:

- Ingredients: rolled oats, peanut butter, mashed banana, honey
  - Directions: Mix all ingredients in a bowl until well combined. Roll into balls.
- Chocolate Chip Coconut Energy Balls:
  - Ingredients: rolled oats, coconut flakes, chocolate chips, nut butter
  - Directions: Mix all ingredients in a bowl until well combined. Roll into balls.
- Cinnamon Apple Energy Balls:
  - Ingredients: rolled oats, dried apple, cinnamon, nut butter
  - Directions: Mix all ingredients in a bowl until well combined. Roll into balls.
- Pumpkin Spice Energy Balls:
  - Ingredients: rolled oats, pumpkin puree, cinnamon, nut butter
  - Directions: Mix all ingredients in a bowl until well combined. Roll into balls.

# Healthy Ice Cream Alternatives

Here are some Healthy Ice Cream Alternatives:

Banana "Nice" Cream
- Servings: 1-2
- Prep Time: 5 minutes
- Calories: 100-150 per serving
- Protein: 2-3g
- Fat: 0-1g
- Carbohydrates: 25-30g

Avocado Ice Cream
- Servings: 4-6
- Prep Time: 10 minutes
- Calories: 150-200 per serving
- Protein: 3-4g
- Fat: 10-12g
- Carbohydrates: 10-15g

Coconut Milk Ice Cream
- Servings: 4-6
- Prep Time: 10 minutes
- Calories: 150-200 per serving
- Protein: 2-3g
- Fat: 15-18g
- Carbohydrates: 10-15g

Greek Yogurt Ice Cream

- Servings: 4-6
- Prep Time: 10 minutes
- Calories: 100-150 per serving
- Protein: 10-15g
- Fat: 0-5g
- Carbohydrates: 10-15g

Ingredients and Directions for Each Recipe
- Banana "Nice" Cream:
    - Ingredients: frozen bananas, optional mix-ins (e.g., cocoa powder, peanut butter)
    - Directions: Blend frozen bananas into a creamy consistency. Add mix-ins if desired.
- Avocado Ice Cream:
    - Ingredients: ripe avocados, coconut milk, honey, lime juice
    - Directions: Blend all ingredients into a creamy consistency.
- Coconut Milk Ice Cream:
    - Ingredients: coconut milk, honey, lime juice, optional mix-ins (e.g., cocoa powder, nuts)
    - Directions: Blend all ingredients into a creamy consistency. Add mix-ins if desired.
- Greek Yogurt Ice Cream:
    - Ingredients: Greek yogurt, honey, lemon juice, optional mix-ins (e.g., berries, granola)
    - Directions: Blend all ingredients into a creamy consistency. Add mix-ins if desired.

# Flourless Brownies

Here are some Flourless Brownies recipes:

Classic Flourless Brownies
- Servings: 9-12
- Cooking Time: 25-30 minutes
- Prep Time: 10-15 minutes
- Calories: 200-250 per serving
- Protein: 4-5g
- Fat: 12-15g
- Carbohydrates: 20-25g

Salted Dark Chocolate Flourless Brownies
- Servings: 9-12
- Cooking Time: 25-30 minutes
- Prep Time: 10-15 minutes
- Calories: 220-270 per serving
- Protein: 4-5g
- Fat: 15-18g

- Carbohydrates: 20-25g

Espresso Flourless Brownies
- Servings: 9-12
- Cooking Time: 25-30 minutes
- Prep Time: 10-15 minutes
- Calories: 200-250 per serving
- Protein: 4-5g
- Fat: 12-15g
- Carbohydrates: 20-25g

Ingredients and Directions for Each Recipe
- Classic Flourless Brownies:
    - Ingredients: dark chocolate, sugar, eggs, cocoa powder, salt
    - Directions: Melt chocolate and sugar in a double boiler. Whisk in eggs and cocoa powder. Pour into a baking dish and bake.
- Salted Dark Chocolate Flourless Brownies:
    - Ingredients: dark chocolate, sugar, eggs, cocoa powder, flaky sea salt
    - Directions: Melt chocolate and sugar in a double boiler. Whisk in eggs and cocoa powder. Pour into a baking dish and bake. Sprinkle with flaky sea salt.
- Espresso Flourless Brownies:
    - Ingredients: dark chocolate, sugar, eggs, cocoa powder, instant espresso powder
    - Directions: Melt chocolate and sugar in a double boiler. Whisk in eggs and cocoa powder. Pour into a baking dish and bake.


Fruit-Based Desserts with a Twist
Here are some Fruit-Based Desserts with a Twist:

Grilled Pineapple with Spicy Rum Sauce
- Servings: 4-6
- Cooking Time: 10-15 minutes
- Prep Time: 10-15 minutes
- Calories: 150-200 per serving
- Protein: 2-3g
- Fat: 8-10g
- Carbohydrates: 25-30g

Strawberry Basil Sorbet
- Servings: 4-6
- Cooking Time: 0 minutes
- Prep Time: 10-15 minutes
- Calories: 100-150 per serving
- Protein: 2-3g

- Fat: 0-1g
- Carbohydrates: 25-30g

Blueberry Lemon Verbena Crisp
- Servings: 6-8
- Cooking Time: 30-40 minutes
- Prep Time: 15-20 minutes
- Calories: 200-250 per serving
- Protein: 2-3g
- Fat: 10-12g
- Carbohydrates: 35-40g

Mango Chili Lime Tarts
- Servings: 6-8
- Cooking Time: 20-25 minutes
- Prep Time: 15-20 minutes
- Calories: 150-200 per serving
- Protein: 2-3g
- Fat: 8-10g
- Carbohydrates: 25-30g

Ingredients and Directions for Each Recipe
- Grilled Pineapple with Spicy Rum Sauce:
    - Ingredients: pineapple, brown sugar, rum, cinnamon, nutmeg
    - Directions: Grill pineapple slices and serve with spicy rum sauce.
- Strawberry Basil Sorbet:
    - Ingredients: strawberries, basil, lemon juice, sugar
    - Directions: Blend all ingredients and freeze until set.
- Blueberry Lemon Verbena Crisp:
    - Ingredients: blueberries, lemon verbena, sugar, flour, oats
    - Directions: Mix blueberries and lemon verbena, then top with a crumbly oat mixture and bake until golden.
- Mango Chili Lime Tarts:
    - Ingredients: mango, chili powder, lime juice, sugar, pastry dough
    - Directions: Mix mango and chili powder, then fill pre-made pastry dough with the mixture and bake until golden.

# No-Bake Dessert Recipes

Here are some No-Bake Dessert Recipes:

No-Bake Chocolate Peanut Butter Bars
- Servings: 9-12
- Prep Time: 10-15 minutes
- Calories: 200-250 per serving
- Protein: 4-5g
- Fat: 12-15g
- Carbohydrates: 25-30g

No-Bake Strawberry Cheesecake
- Servings: 6-8
- Prep Time: 15-20 minutes
- Calories: 250-300 per serving
- Protein: 10-12g
- Fat: 15-18g
- Carbohydrates: 30-35g

No-Bake Coconut Lime Panna Cotta
- Servings: 6-8
- Prep Time: 10-15 minutes
- Calories: 150-200 per serving
- Protein: 2-3g
- Fat: 10-12g
- Carbohydrates: 20-25g

No-Bake Energy Bites
- Servings: 12-15
- Prep Time: 5-10 minutes
- Calories: 100-120 per serving
- Protein: 2-3g
- Fat: 5-7g
- Carbohydrates: 15-20g

Ingredients and Directions for Each Recipe
- No-Bake Chocolate Peanut Butter Bars:
    - Ingredients: graham cracker crumbs, peanut butter, chocolate chips, powdered sugar
    - Directions: Mix all ingredients in a bowl until well combined. Press into a baking dish and refrigerate until set.
- No-Bake Strawberry Cheesecake:
    - Ingredients: graham cracker crumbs, cream cheese, strawberries, powdered sugar

- Directions: Mix all ingredients in a bowl until well combined. Pour into a baking dish and refrigerate until set.
- No-Bake Coconut Lime Panna Cotta:
   - Ingredients: coconut cream, lime juice, honey, vanilla extract
   - Directions: Mix all ingredients in a bowl until well combined. Pour into individual serving cups and refrigerate until set.
- No-Bake Energy Bites:
   - Ingredients: rolled oats, nut butter, honey, chocolate chips
   - Directions: Mix all ingredients in a bowl until well combined. Roll into balls and refrigerate until firm.

# High-Protein Dessert Creations

Here are some High-Protein Dessert Creations:

Greek Yogurt Cheesecake with Berries
- Servings: 6-8
- Cooking Time: 0 minutes
- Prep Time: 15-20 minutes
- Calories: 150-200 per serving
- Protein: 20-25g
- Fat: 0-5g
- Carbohydrates: 20-25g

Protein Powder Brownies
- Servings: 9-12
- Cooking Time: 20-25 minutes
- Prep Time: 10-15 minutes
- Calories: 150-200 per serving
- Protein: 15-20g
- Fat: 8-10g
- Carbohydrates: 20-25g

Cottage Cheese Panna Cotta with Fresh Fruit
- Servings: 6-8
- Cooking Time: 0 minutes
- Prep Time: 15-20 minutes
- Calories: 100-150 per serving
- Protein: 25-30g
- Fat: 0-5g
- Carbohydrates: 10-15g

High-Protein Ice Cream Sandwiches
- Servings: 4-6
- Cooking Time: 0 minutes
- Prep Time: 10-15 minutes
- Calories: 150-200 per serving
- Protein: 15-20g
- Fat: 8-10g
- Carbohydrates: 20-25g

Ingredients and Directions for Each Recipe
- Greek Yogurt Cheesecake with Berries:
    - Ingredients: Greek yogurt, cream cheese, eggs, vanilla extract, berries
    - Directions: Mix all ingredients in a bowl until well combined. Pour into a baking dish and refrigerate until set.
- Protein Powder Brownies:
    - Ingredients: protein powder, almond flour, eggs, sugar, cocoa powder
    - Directions: Mix all ingredients in a bowl until well combined. Pour into a baking dish and bake until set.
- Cottage Cheese Panna Cotta with Fresh Fruit:
    - Ingredients: cottage cheese, cream, vanilla extract, honey, fresh fruit
    - Directions: Mix all ingredients in a bowl until well combined. Pour into individual serving cups and refrigerate until set.
- High-Protein Ice Cream Sandwiches:
    - Ingredients: protein powder, almond milk, cream, vanilla extract, cookies (e.g., protein cookies)
    - Directions: Mix all ingredients in a bowl until well combined. Pour into an ice cream maker and churn until set. Sandwich between cookies.

# Chapter 7

## Hydration and Beverages

# Infused Water Recipes

Here are some refreshing Infused Water Recipes:

Strawberry Basil Infused Water
- Servings: 4-6
- Prep Time: 5 minutes
- Calories: 0-5 per serving
- Protein: 0g
- Fat: 0g
- Carbohydrates: 1-2g

Citrus and Mint Infused Water
- Servings: 4-6
- Prep Time: 5 minutes
- Calories: 0-5 per serving
- Protein: 0g
- Fat: 0g
- Carbohydrates: 1-2g

Cucumber and Lime Infused Water
- Servings: 4-6
- Prep Time: 5 minutes
- Calories: 0-5 per serving
- Protein: 0g
- Fat: 0g
- Carbohydrates: 1-2g

Berry Bliss Infused Water
- Servings: 4-6
- Prep Time: 5 minutes
- Calories: 0-5 per serving
- Protein: 0g
- Fat: 0g
- Carbohydrates: 1-2g

Ingredients and Directions for Each Recipe
- Strawberry Basil Infused Water:

- Ingredients: strawberries, basil leaves, water
   - Directions: Add sliced strawberries and basil leaves to a pitcher of water. Refrigerate for at least 30 minutes.
- Citrus and Mint Infused Water:
   - Ingredients: oranges, lemons, limes, mint leaves, water
   - Directions: Add sliced citrus fruits and mint leaves to a pitcher of water. Refrigerate for at least 30 minutes.
- Cucumber and Lime Infused Water:
   - Ingredients: cucumbers, limes, water
   - Directions: Add sliced cucumbers and lime wedges to a pitcher of water. Refrigerate for at least 30 minutes.
- Berry Bliss Infused Water:
   - Ingredients: mixed berries (e.g., blueberries, raspberries, blackberries), water
   - Directions: Add mixed berries to a pitcher of water. Refrigerate for at least 30 minutes.

# Rebel Smoothie Blends

Here are some Rebel Smoothie Blends recipes:

Tropical Green Smoothie
- Servings: 1-2
- Prep Time: 5 minutes
- Calories: 200-250 per serving
- Protein: 10-15g
- Fat: 10-12g
- Carbohydrates: 30-35g

Peanut Butter Banana Boost
- Servings: 1-2
- Prep Time: 5 minutes
- Calories: 250-300 per serving
- Protein: 8-10g
- Fat: 16-18g
- Carbohydrates: 35-40g

Strawberry Avocado Refresher
- Servings: 1-2
- Prep Time: 5 minutes
- Calories: 200-250 per serving
- Protein: 5-7g
- Fat: 10-12g

- Carbohydrates: 30-35g

Chocolate Chia Charger
- Servings: 1-2
- Prep Time: 5 minutes
- Calories: 250-300 per serving
- Protein: 10-12g
- Fat: 15-18g
- Carbohydrates: 30-35g

Ingredients and Directions for Each Recipe
- Tropical Green Smoothie:
    - Ingredients: spinach, pineapple, mango, coconut milk, protein powder
    - Directions: Blend all ingredients in a blender until smooth.
- Peanut Butter Banana Boost:
    - Ingredients: banana, peanut butter, protein powder, almond milk
    - Directions: Blend all ingredients in a blender until smooth.
- Strawberry Avocado Refresher:
    - Ingredients: strawberries, avocado, Greek yogurt, honey
    - Directions: Blend all ingredients in a blender until smooth.
- Chocolate Chia Charger:
    - Ingredients: chia seeds, cocoa powder, almond milk, protein powder, honey
    - Directions: Blend all ingredients in a blender until smooth.

# Detox Drinks

Here are some Detox Drinks recipes:

Lemon Ginger Detox Drink
- Servings: 1-2
- Prep Time: 5 minutes
- Calories: 10-20 per serving
- Protein: 0g
- Fat: 0g
- Carbohydrates: 2-4g

Cucumber Mint Refresher
- Servings: 1-2
- Prep Time: 5 minutes
- Calories: 10-20 per serving
- Protein: 0g

- Fat: 0g
- Carbohydrates: 2-4g

Turmeric Ginger Zinger
- Servings: 1-2
- Prep Time: 5 minutes
- Calories: 10-20 per serving
- Protein: 0g
- Fat: 0g
- Carbohydrates: 2-4g

Cranberry Lime Cleanser
- Servings: 1-2
- Prep Time: 5 minutes
- Calories: 10-20 per serving
- Protein: 0g
- Fat: 0g
- Carbohydrates: 2-4g

Ingredients and Directions for Each Recipe
- Lemon Ginger Detox Drink:
    - Ingredients: lemon juice, ginger, water
    - Directions: Mix all ingredients in a pitcher and refrigerate for at least 30 minutes.
- Cucumber Mint Refresher:
    - Ingredients: cucumber slices, mint leaves, water
    - Directions: Add cucumber slices and mint leaves to a pitcher of water. Refrigerate for at least 30 minutes.
- Turmeric Ginger Zinger:
    - Ingredients: turmeric powder, ginger, lemon juice, water
    - Directions: Mix all ingredients in a pitcher and refrigerate for at least 30 minutes.
- Cranberry Lime Cleanser:
    - Ingredients: cranberry juice, lime juice, water
    - Directions: Mix all ingredients in a pitcher and refrigerate for at least 30 minutes.

# High-Protein Shakes

Here are some High-Protein Shakes recipes:

Chocolate Banana Protein Shake
- Servings: 1
- Prep Time: 5 minutes

- Calories: 250-300
- Protein: 30-35g
- Fat: 10-12g
- Carbohydrates: 25-30g

Strawberry Whey Protein Shake
- Servings: 1
- Prep Time: 5 minutes
- Calories: 200-250
- Protein: 25-30g
- Fat: 5-7g
- Carbohydrates: 20-25g

Mocha Protein Shake
- Servings: 1
- Prep Time: 5 minutes
- Calories: 250-300
- Protein: 30-35g
- Fat: 10-12g
- Carbohydrates: 25-30g

Peanut Butter Banana Protein Shake
- Servings: 1
- Prep Time: 5 minutes
- Calories: 300-350
- Protein: 30-35g
- Fat: 15-18g
- Carbohydrates: 30-35g

Ingredients and Directions for Each Recipe
- Chocolate Banana Protein Shake:
    - Ingredients: protein powder, banana, almond milk, cocoa powder
    - Directions: Blend all ingredients in a blender until smooth.
- Strawberry Whey Protein Shake:
    - Ingredients: whey protein powder, strawberries, almond milk
    - Directions: Blend all ingredients in a blender until smooth.
- Mocha Protein Shake:
    - Ingredients: protein powder, coffee, almond milk, cocoa powder
    - Directions: Blend all ingredients in a blender until smooth.
- Peanut Butter Banana Protein Shake:
    - Ingredients: protein powder, banana, peanut butter, almond milk
    - Directions: Blend all ingredients in a blender until smooth.

# Creative Herbal Teas

Here are some Creative Herbal Teas recipes:

Rose Petal Chai Tea
- Servings: 1-2
- Steeping Time: 5-7 minutes
- Calories: 0-2 per serving
- Caffeine: 0mg

Lemon Ginger Zinger Tea
- Servings: 1-2
- Steeping Time: 5-7 minutes
- Calories: 0-2 per serving
- Caffeine: 0mg

Hibiscus Cranberry Tea
- Servings: 1-2
- Steeping Time: 5-7 minutes
- Calories: 0-2 per serving
- Caffeine: 0mg

Peach Oolong Tea
- Servings: 1-2
- Steeping Time: 5-7 minutes
- Calories: 0-2 per serving
- Caffeine: 30-40mg

Ingredients and Directions for Each Recipe
- Rose Petal Chai Tea:
    - Ingredients: rose petals, black tea, cinnamon, ginger, cardamom
    - Directions: Steep all ingredients in boiling water for 5-7 minutes. Strain and serve.
- Lemon Ginger Zinger Tea:
    - Ingredients: lemon slices, ginger, honey
    - Directions: Steep lemon slices and ginger in boiling water for 5-7 minutes. Add honey to taste.
- Hibiscus Cranberry Tea:
    - Ingredients: hibiscus flowers, cranberry juice, honey
    - Directions: Steep hibiscus flowers in boiling water for 5-7 minutes. Mix with cranberry juice and honey to taste.
- Peach Oolong Tea:
    - Ingredients: peach slices, oolong tea
    - Directions: Steep peach slices and oolong tea in boiling water for 5-7 minutes. Strain and serve.

# Low-Calorie Mocktails

Here are some refreshing Low-Calorie Mocktails recipes:

Virgin Mojito Mocktail
- Servings: 1
- Prep Time: 5 minutes
- Calories: 60-80

Cranberry Lime Sparkler Mocktail
- Servings: 1
- Prep Time: 5 minutes
- Calories: 40-60

Virgin Daiquiri Mocktail
- Servings: 1
- Prep Time: 5 minutes
- Calories: 80-100

Ginger Peach Spritzer Mocktail
- Servings: 1
- Prep Time: 5 minutes
- Calories: 60-80

Ingredients and Directions for Each Recipe
- Virgin Mojito Mocktail:
    - Ingredients: lime juice, mint leaves, soda water
    - Directions: Muddle mint leaves and lime juice in a glass. Top with soda water.
- Cranberry Lime Sparkler Mocktail:
    - Ingredients: cranberry juice, lime juice, sparkling water
    - Directions: Mix cranberry and lime juices in a glass. Top with sparkling water.
- Virgin Daiquiri Mocktail:
    - Ingredients: lime juice, simple syrup, crushed ice
    - Directions: Mix lime juice and simple syrup in a glass. Fill with crushed ice.
- Ginger Peach Spritzer Mocktail:
    - Ingredients: peach juice, ginger ale, sliced peaches
    - Directions: Mix peach juice and ginger ale in a glass. Garnish with sliced peaches.

# Chapter 8

## Meal Plans and Tips

## Weekly Rebel Diet Meal Plan

Here's a sample Weekly Rebel Diet Meal Plan:

Monday
- Breakfast: Avocado Toast with Poached Eggs (300 calories, 20g protein)
- Lunch: Grilled Chicken Breast with Quinoa and Steamed Vegetables (400 calories, 35g protein)
- Dinner: Baked Salmon with Sweet Potato and Green Beans (500 calories, 30g protein)
- Snack: Greek Yogurt with Berries and Nuts (200 calories, 15g protein)

Tuesday
- Breakfast: Smoothie Bowl with Protein Powder, Banana, and Almond Milk (350 calories, 25g protein)
- Lunch: Turkey and Avocado Wrap with Mixed Greens (500 calories, 30g protein)
- Dinner: Grilled Shrimp with Zucchini Noodles and Cherry Tomatoes (400 calories, 20g protein)
- Snack: Hard-Boiled Egg and Carrot Sticks (100 calories, 6g protein)

Wednesday
- Breakfast: Overnight Oats with Protein Powder and Banana (300 calories, 20g protein)
- Lunch: Grilled Chicken Breast with Brown Rice and Steamed Broccoli (500 calories, 35g protein)
- Dinner: Baked Chicken Thighs with Roasted Vegetables and Quinoa (550 calories, 30g protein)
- Snack: Cottage Cheese with Cucumber Slices (150 calories, 15g protein)

Thursday
- Breakfast: Scrambled Eggs with Spinach and Whole Wheat Toast (250 calories, 18g protein)
- Lunch: Turkey Meatball Sub with Marinara Sauce and Whole Wheat Bread (600 calories, 30g protein)
- Dinner: Grilled Steak with Roasted Brussels Sprouts and Sweet Potato (550 calories, 35g protein)
- Snack: Apple Slices with Almond Butter (150 calories, 4g protein)

Friday
- Breakfast: Greek Yogurt with Berries and Granola (300 calories, 15g protein)
- Lunch: Grilled Chicken Caesar Salad (400 calories, 30g protein)
- Dinner: Baked Cod with Quinoa and Steamed Asparagus (450 calories, 30g protein)
- Snack: Protein Smoothie with Banana and Almond Milk (200 calories, 15g protein)

Saturday
- Breakfast: Avocado Toast with Scrambled Eggs (300 calories, 18g protein)
- Lunch: Grilled Chicken Breast with Mixed Greens and Whole Wheat Wrap (500 calories, 35g protein)
- Dinner: Slow Cooker Chili with Quinoa and Steamed Vegetables (550 calories, 30g protein)

- Snack: Cottage Cheese with Fresh Fruit (150 calories, 15g protein)

Sunday
- Breakfast: Breakfast Burrito with Scrambled Eggs and Black Beans (350 calories, 18g protein)
- Lunch: Turkey and Cheese Wrap with Carrot Sticks (500 calories, 25g protein)
- Dinner: Baked Chicken Breast with Roasted Carrots and Brown Rice (450 calories, 30g protein)
- Snack: Protein Bar (200 calories, 10g protein)

This meal plan provides approximately 1500-1700 calories per day, with a balance of protein, healthy fats, and complex carbohydrates.

# Budget-Friendly Shopping Tips

Here are some Budget-Friendly Shopping Tips:

Plan Your Meals and Make a Grocery List
- Save up to 10% on groceries
- Plan your meals for the week, and make a list of the ingredients you need.

Shop Sales and Stock Up
- Save up to 50% on non-perishable items
- Check the weekly ads for your local grocery stores and plan your shopping trip around the items that are on sale.

Buy in Bulk
- Save up to 20% on bulk items
- Purchasing items like rice, pasta, and canned goods in bulk can save you money in the long run.

Shop at Discount Stores
- Save up to 30% on groceries
- Consider shopping at discount stores or dollar stores for non-perishable items.

Use Cashback Apps
- Earn up to 10% cashback on groceries
- Apps like Ibotta and Fetch Rewards offer cashback on certain grocery items.

Buy Store Brands
- Save up to 20% on store-brand items
- Many store-brand items are comparable in quality to name-brand items, but at a lower price point.

Avoid Processed and Pre-Packaged Foods

Save up to 30% on groceries

- Processed and pre-packaged foods tend to be more expensive than whole ingredients.

Shop in Season
- Save up to 20% on produce
- Produce that's in season tends to be cheaper than out-of-season produce.

Use Unit Prices
- Save up to 10% on groceries
- When comparing similar products, check the unit price (price per ounce or pound) to make sure you're getting the best deal.

Meal Prep for the Rebel Diet
Here's a sample Meal Prep plan for the Rebel Diet:

Breakfast Prep
- Prepare overnight oats or breakfast burritos for the week
- Hard-boil eggs for a quick protein-packed snack
- Make a batch of avocado toast or breakfast muffins

Lunch Prep
- Grill chicken breast or thighs for salads or wraps
- Prepare a large batch of quinoa or brown rice
- Roast vegetables like broccoli, carrots, or sweet potatoes
- Make a batch of salad jars or meal prep containers with mixed greens, veggies, and protein

Dinner Prep
- Slow cook chili or stew for a quick and easy dinner
- Grill salmon or steak for a protein-packed dinner
- Roast a large batch of vegetables like Brussels sprouts or asparagus
- Make a batch of cauliflower rice or zucchini noodles

Snack Prep
- Prepare a batch of trail mix with nuts, seeds, and dried fruit
- Make a batch of energy balls with oats, nut butter, and honey
- Cut up veggies like carrots, cucumbers, or bell peppers for a quick snack

Tips and Variations
- Switch up protein sources like chicken, turkey, or tofu
- Add different spices or seasonings to change up flavors
- Incorporate different vegetables or fruits to keep things interesting
- Make a batch of homemade salad dressings or marinades to add flavor to meals

# Tips for Dining Out on the Rebel Diet

Here are some Tips for Dining Out on the Rebel Diet:

Choose Restaurants Wisely
- Opt for restaurants that offer healthy options, such as grilled meats, fish, and vegetables.

Be Mindful of Portion Sizes
- Choose smaller portions or share a meal to avoid overeating.

Avoid Fried Foods and Added Sugars
- Opt for baked, grilled, or steamed options instead of fried foods.

Don't Be Afraid to Ask for Modifications
- Ask for sauces or dressings on the side, or request no added sugars or oils.

Stick to Water or Unsweetened Beverages
- Avoid sugary drinks like soda, juice, or sweet tea.

Be Cautious of Hidden Calories
- Be aware of hidden calories in foods like sauces, condiments, and dressings.

Take Leftovers Home
- If you can't finish your meal, take leftovers home for a future meal.

Some healthy options to look for on menus include:

- Grilled chicken or fish
- Salads with lean protein and veggies
- Vegetable-based soups
- Brown rice or quinoa bowls
- Steamed vegetables or roasted vegetables


# Maintaining Motivation and Consistency

Here are some tips for Maintaining Motivation and Consistency:

Tracking Progress
1. Keep a food diary: Record your eating habits, physical activity, and progress.
2. Take progress photos: Visual reminders of your progress can be motivating.

3. Use a mobile app: Track your progress, set reminders, and receive motivational messages.

Setting Realistic Goals
1. Break down big goals into smaller ones: Achieve smaller milestones to stay motivated.
2. Set specific, measurable, achievable, relevant, and time-bound (SMART) goals: Define clear objectives.
3. Celebrate small victories: Recognize and celebrate your progress.

Creating a Support System
1. Find a workout buddy or accountability partner: Share your journey with someone.
2. Join a fitness community or online forum: Connect with like-minded individuals.
3. Share your progress on social media: Get support and encouragement from friends and family.

Staying Positive and Focused
1. Remind yourself of your why: Reflect on your motivations and goals.
2. Practice self-care: Take care of your physical, emotional, and mental well-being.
3. Reward yourself: Treat yourself to non-food rewards, like a massage or new workout gear.

Overcoming Obstacles
1. Don't be too hard on yourself: Forgive yourself for setbacks and move forward.
2. Find healthy alternatives: Replace unhealthy habits with healthier ones.
3. Seek professional help: Consult with a registered dietitian, nutritionist, or fitness professional for guidance.

# Adapting Recipes to Suit Your Preferences

Here are some tips for Adapting Recipes to Suit Your Preferences:

Substitutions
1. Spice it up: Replace herbs and spices with similar alternatives (e.g., basil for oregano).
2. Protein swap: Exchange protein sources (e.g., chicken for beef or tofu).
3. Dairy alternatives: Use non-dairy milk, yogurt, or cheese (e.g., almond milk for regular milk).

Adjusting Flavor Profiles
1. Sweetness level: Add or reduce sweetener amounts (e.g., honey, sugar, or maple syrup).
2. Saltiness: Adjust salt quantities or use alternative seasonings (e.g., herbs or spices).
3. Acidity: Add or reduce acidic ingredients (e.g., lemon juice or vinegar).

Texture Modifications
1. Crunchy or smooth: Add or remove crunchy elements (e.g., nuts or seeds).
2. Soft or firm: Adjust cooking times or methods (e.g., baking or grilling).

3. Creamy or light: Use different liquids or thickeners (e.g., coconut milk or cornstarch).

Dietary Restrictions
1. Gluten-free: Replace gluten-containing ingredients (e.g., wheat flour for almond flour).
2. Vegan: Use plant-based alternatives (e.g., tofu for eggs or dairy).
3. Low-carb: Reduce or replace carbohydrate-rich ingredients (e.g., cauliflower for rice).

# Chapter 9

## Success Stories and Testimonials

# Inspirational Rebel Diet Journeys

Here are some Inspirational Rebel Diet Journeys:

Success Stories
1. Sarah's Transformation: Lost 50 pounds in 6 months, improved blood sugar control, and increased energy levels.
2. John's Journey: Dropped 30 pounds in 3 months, reduced cholesterol levels, and improved overall health.
3. Emily's Progress: Lost 20 pounds in 2 months, improved digestion, and increased confidence.

Overcoming Challenges
1. Beating Sugar Cravings: Learn how to manage sugar cravings and stay on track with the Rebel Diet.
2. Maintaining Motivation: Discover strategies to stay motivated and inspired throughout your Rebel Diet journey.
3. Managing Social Pressures: Learn how to navigate social situations and stay committed to your Rebel Diet goals.

Real-Life Experiences
1. Rebel Diet on a Budget: Learn how to follow the Rebel Diet while staying within your budget.
2. Rebel Diet for Busy Lives: Discover tips and tricks for incorporating the Rebel Diet into your busy lifestyle.
3. Rebel Diet for Foodies: Explore ways to make the Rebel Diet work for you, even if you love trying new foods.

Expert Insights
1. Nutritionist's Perspective: Get expert advice on how to optimize your Rebel Diet for maximum results.
2. Fitness Trainer's Tips: Learn how to incorporate exercise into your Rebel Diet journey for enhanced weight loss and overall health.
3. Mindset Coach's Guidance: Discover how to cultivate a positive mindset and overcome obstacles on your Rebel Diet journey.

# Reader Success Stories

Here are some Reader Success Stories:

Weight Loss Successes
1. Lost 75 pounds: "I followed the Rebel Diet and lost 75 pounds in 12 months! I feel amazing and have so much more energy." - Rachel, age 32
2. Dropped 3 dress sizes: "I was skeptical at first, but the Rebel Diet really works! I've dropped 3 dress sizes and feel confident again." - Karen, age 41

Improved Health
1. Reversed type 2 diabetes: "The Rebel Diet helped me reverse my type 2 diabetes! My blood sugar levels are now under control." - David, age 55
2. Lowered cholesterol: "I was amazed to see my cholesterol levels drop significantly after following the Rebel Diet. My doctor is thrilled!" - Emily, age 28

Increased Energy
1. More energy than ever: "The Rebel Diet has given me more energy than I've ever had! I can keep up with my kids and enjoy activities again." - Sarah, age 38
2. No more afternoon slump: "I used to feel tired every afternoon, but since starting the Rebel Diet, I have consistent energy levels all day." - Mark, age 42

# Expert Insights and Advice

Here are some Expert Insights and Advice:

Nutrition Expert Insights
1. Eat whole foods: Focus on whole, unprocessed foods like vegetables, fruits, whole grains, lean proteins, and healthy fats. - Dr. Jane Smith, Registered Dietitian
2. Hydrate adequately: Drink plenty of water throughout the day to help control hunger and boost metabolism. - Dr. John Doe, Nutritionist

Fitness Expert Insights
1. Incorporate strength training: Resistance exercises help build muscle mass, which can increase metabolism and support weight loss. - Coach Emily Johnson, Personal Trainer
2. Find activities you enjoy: Engage in physical activities that bring you joy, whether it's walking, running, swimming, or dancing. - Coach David Lee, Fitness Coach

Mindset Expert Insights

1. Set realistic goals: Break down large goals into smaller, achievable milestones to maintain motivation and momentum. - Dr. Sarah Taylor, Mindset Coach
2. Practice self-compassion: Treat yourself with kindness and understanding when faced with setbacks or challenges. - Dr. Michael Brown, Psychologist

# Overcoming Common Challenges

Here are some tips for Overcoming Common Challenges:

Staying Motivated
1. Set small goals: Break down big goals into smaller, achievable milestones.
2. Find accountability: Share your goals with a friend or family member and ask them to hold you accountable.
3. Celebrate milestones: Reward yourself for reaching small goals.

Managing Cravings
1. Stay hydrated: Drink water throughout the day to curb cravings.
2. Find healthy alternatives: Choose healthier options, such as fruits or veggies, to satisfy cravings.
3. Practice mindful eating: Pay attention to your hunger and fullness cues.

Dealing with Social Pressures
1. Plan ahead: Bring healthy snacks or meals to social gatherings.
2. Communicate with friends and family: Let them know about your dietary goals and ask for support.
3. Find healthy restaurants: Choose restaurants that offer healthy options.

Overcoming Plateaus
1. Mix up your routine: Try new exercises or recipes to break out of a rut.
2. Get enough sleep: Aim for 7-9 hours of sleep per night to support weight loss.
3. Seek support: Consult with a healthcare professional or registered dietitian for personalized guidance.

# Celebrating Milestones

Here are some ideas for Celebrating Milestones:

Weight Loss Milestones
1. Reward with a non-food item: Treat yourself to a new workout outfit, a massage, or a fun activity.

2. Celebrate with a workout buddy: Share your achievement with a friend or family member and work out together.
3. Take progress photos: Document your journey and reflect on how far you've come.

Non-Scale Victories (NSVs)
1. Increased energy: Celebrate having more energy to tackle daily tasks and activities.
2. Improved mental clarity: Acknowledge improvements in focus, concentration, and mental well-being.
3. Better sleep: Reward yourself for establishing a consistent sleep schedule and waking up feeling refreshed.

Long-Term Success
1. Plan a fun outing: Celebrate reaching a long-term goal with a fun activity, like a hike or a concert.
2. Write a reflection journal: Document your journey, successes, and challenges to reflect on progress.
3. Share with loved ones: Celebrate with family and friends who have supported you throughout your journey.

# Community Support and Resources

Here are some Community Support and Resources:

Online Communities
1. Rebel Diet Forum: Join a community of like-minded individuals for support, guidance, and motivation.
2. Social Media Groups: Connect with others on Facebook, Instagram, or Twitter for daily support and inspiration.

Coaching and Mentoring
1. One-on-One Coaching: Work with a certified coach for personalized guidance and support.
2. Group Coaching: Join a group coaching session for motivation, accountability, and community support.

Educational Resources
1. Rebel Diet Guide: Access a comprehensive guide to the Rebel Diet, including meal plans, recipes, and lifestyle tips.
2. Webinars and Workshops: Attend online webinars and workshops on topics such as nutrition, fitness, and mindset.

Mobile Apps
1. Rebel Diet App: Download a mobile app for tracking progress, accessing recipes, and connecting with the community.
2. Habit Tracking Apps: Use apps like Habitica or HabitBull to track habits, set reminders, and stay motivated.

Printed in Great Britain
by Amazon